# Google Pixel 9a 5G U

# For Beginners Seniors

## A Complete Step-by-Step User Guide – Simplified for Effortless Mastery, with Tips and Tricks for Setup & Configuration

Maryland J. Stones

## Table of Contents

Chapter 1: Introduction to Your Google Pixel 9a ..................................................20

Overview of the Google Pixel 9a..........20

Key Features and Specifications ..........20

What's in the Box? ..............................22

Getting Started with Your Pixel 9a .........24

Insert the SIM Card: ............................24

Power On Your Phone: ........................24

Set Up Your Phone:.............................25

Finish the Setup:................................26

Chapter 2: Setting Up Your Google Pixel 9a ..........................................................27

Inserting the SIM Card and microSD (if applicable)..........................................27

Inserting the SIM Card:........................28

Powering On Your Pixel 9a...................29

Initial Setup Guide ..............................29

1. Select your Language:......................30

2. Connect to Wi-Fi: ...........................30

3. Sign in to Your Google Account: .......31

Why is signing in to your Google account important? .................................... 31

Transferring Data from Your Old Device ......................................................... 32

Option 1: Using a Cable (Recommended for Fast Transfer) .................................. 32

Option 2: Using Google Backup (No Cable Needed) ......................................... 33

Setting Up Google Services .................. 34

1. Google Assistant: ........................... 34

2. Google Pay: ...................................... 35

3. Google Cloud Backup: ....................... 35

Chapter 3: Navigating the Google Pixel 9a .................................................... 37

Understanding the Home Screen and Its Layout ................................................... 37

Key Components: ................................. 38

Navigating Using Gestures .................. 39

Basic Gestures: .................................... 39

Go to the Home Screen: ....................... 39

Switch Between Apps: ......................... 40

Go Back: ................................40

Open Google Assistant:....................40

Using the Status Bar and Quick Settings ............................. 41

Quick Settings: ...........................42

Customizing Your Home Screen.......... 43

1. Change Your Wallpaper: ................44

2. Move or Remove Apps: ...................44

3. Create Folders: .........................45

4. Add Widgets: ............................45

Managing Notifications and Widgets .46

Managing Notifications:....................46

Chapter 4: Connecting to Wi-Fi and Mobile Networks...............................49

Connecting to Wi-Fi Networks............49

Steps to Connect to Wi-Fi: ..................49

Managing Wi-Fi Settings ....................51

Advanced Wi-Fi Settings:....................51

Setting Up Mobile Data and Roaming 53

Enable Mobile Data: ..........................54

Setting Up Roaming: ..........................55

Using Airplane Mode .......................... 55

Turning on Airplane Mode: ................. 56

Connecting to Bluetooth Devices........ 57

Connecting to Bluetooth: .................... 57

Setting Up a VPN Connection ............. 58

Setting Up a VPN:.............................. 59

Chapter 5: Making Calls and Sending
Messages ..................................................61

Making and Receiving Voice Calls........61

Making a Call:.......................................61

Receiving a Call:.................................. 62

Managing Contacts and Favorites ....... 63

Adding a New Contact: ........................ 63

Marking Favorites:................................ 63

Using Google Assistant for Hands-Free
Calling ..................................................64

Sending Text Messages via SMS, MMS,
and RCS.................................................. 65

Sending an SMS or MMS: .................... 65

Using Google Messages for Chat
Features.................................................67

Setting Up Voicemail ...............68

Accessing Voicemail: ...............69

Chapter 6: Using the Camera ...............70

Overview of the Pixel 9a's Camera Features ...............70

Taking Photos with the Rear and Front Camera ...............71

Using Night Sight, Portrait Mode, and Other Special Camera Modes ...............72

Portrait Mode: ...............72

Other Camera Modes: ...............73

Recording Videos ...............73

Editing and Sharing Photos/Videos ....73

Using Google Photos for Backups and Organization ...............74

Chapter 7: Using Google Assistant ...............76

What is Google Assistant? ...............76

Activating and Customizing Google Assistant ...............77

Activating Google Assistant: ...............77

Customizing Google Assistant: ...............78

Using Voice Commands to Control Your
Device.................................................. 79

Make Calls:......................................... 79

Send Text Messages: ...........................80

Control Music and Media: ..................80

Set Reminders and Alarms:.................80

Get Directions:....................................81

Integrating Google Assistant with Other
Apps ....................................................81

Connecting Smart Home Devices: .......81

Third-Party App Integration:.............. 82

Creating Routines for Everyday Tasks. 82

Setting Up a Routine: .......................... 83

Example of a Morning Routine:...........84

Using Google Assistant for Hands-Free
Navigation...........................................84

Getting Directions:............................. 85

Control Navigation During the Trip:... 85

Chapter 8: Setting Up and Using Apps ..86

Downloading Apps from Google Play
Store ...................................................86

Steps to Download an App:...............86

Managing Installed Apps ................87

Viewing Installed Apps: .................87

Updating Apps:.............................87

Checking App Details:....................88

Using Google Play Services and
Subscriptions ...............................88

Managing Subscriptions: ...............88

Google Play Services:.....................89

Organizing Apps into Folders.............89

Creating an App Folder: .................89

Adding More Apps to a Folder:...........90

Managing App Permissions ...............90

Uninstalling Apps ........................ 91

Steps to Uninstall an App:............... 91

Chapter 9: Managing Battery Life...........92

Checking Battery Status and Health ...92

Power-Saving Modes and Settings.......92

Tips to Extend Battery Life..................93

Charging Your Google Pixel 9a (Wired
and Wireless) .................................93

Wired Charging:....................................94

Wireless Charging:............................94

Using Battery Optimization Features .94

Understanding Fast Charging and
Adaptive Charging...............................95

Adaptive Charging:..........................95

Chapter 10: Data and Security................96

Setting Up a Secure Lock Screen (PIN,
Pattern, Password) .............................96

Steps to Set Up a Lock Screen:.............96

Using Fingerprint and Facial
Recognition for Security ....................97

Setting Up Fingerprint Unlock:...........97

Setting Up Face Unlock:......................98

Setting Up Google Find My Device .....98

Steps to Set Up Find My Device:..........99

Managing App Permissions and Privacy
Settings.................................................99

Backing Up and Restoring Your Data.100

Steps to Backup Your Data:..................100

Steps to Restore Your Data:..................100

Using Two-Factor Authentication for
Google Services ........................... 101

Steps to Enable Two-Factor
Authentication: ........................... 101

Chapter 11: Managing Storage and Files 103

Checking Available Storage on Your
Pixel 9a ...................................103

Moving Files Between Internal Storage
and SD Card (if applicable) ............... 104

Steps to Move Files: ........................ 104

Using Google Drive for Cloud Storage
.......................................... 104

Steps to Upload Files to Google Drive:
..........................................105

Managing Files with the Files App .....105

Features of the Files App: ..................105

Deleting Files and Managing Space .. 106

Steps to Delete Files: ...................... 106

Using Google Photos for Photo and
Video Storage ............................. 106

Steps to Backup Photos: .................. 106

Chapter 12: Customizing Your Google Pixel 9a ...................................108

Changing the Wallpaper and Themes108

Steps to Change Wallpaper: ................108

Customizing the Lock Screen and Home Screen Settings ..................................109

To Customize the Home Screen: ........109

Adjusting System Font, Display, and Animation Speed ................................109

Steps to Adjust Display: ......................109

Setting Up Dark Mode and Other Display Settings .................................. 110

Steps to Enable Dark Mode: ............... 110

Sound and Notification Settings ......... 111

Adjusting Sound Settings: ................... 111

Creating Custom Shortcuts for Apps .. 111

Steps to Create a Shortcut: ................... 111

Chapter 13: Advanced Features ..............112

Using the Google Pixel 9a with a Smart Home Setup ..........................................112

Setting Up Digital Wellbeing and Focus Mode.............. 112

Steps to Set Up Focus Mode:...............113

Managing Screen Time and App Limits ...................................................113

Setting Up Gesture Navigation and Customizing It ...................................113

Using Google Lens for Visual Search...113

Exploring the Pixel 9a's "Now Playing" Feature.................................. 114

Chapter 14: Connectivity with Other Devices ...................................115

Connecting Pixel 9a to a TV or Projector Using Chromecast ...............................115

Steps to Use Chromecast:...................115

Using the Google Pixel 9a as a Hotspot ............................................. 116

Steps to Set Up a Mobile Hotspot:...... 116

Setting Up USB OTG to Connect External Devices ................................. 117

Steps to Use USB OTG:....................... 118

Pairing Pixel 9a with Wearables (Google Fit, Wear OS Devices) ......................... 118

Steps to Pair with Wear OS Devices: .. 118

Sharing Files Using Nearby Share ...... 119

Using Android Auto in Your Car ........ 120

Steps to Set Up Android Auto: ............. 121

Chapter 15: Troubleshooting and FAQs. 123

Common Issues and Fixes (Wi-Fi Problems, App Crashes, etc.) .............. 123

Wi-Fi Problems: ................................... 123

App Crashes: ........................................ 124

What to Do if Your Pixel 9a Freezes or is Unresponsive ...................................... 124

Steps to Force Restart: ......................... 124

Restoring Your Google Pixel 9a to Factory Settings ................................... 125

Steps to Perform a Factory Reset: ....... 125

What to Do if Your Phone is Not Charging ............................................. 126

Contacting Google Support ................. 126

How to Contact Google Support: ........ 127

Chapter 16: Software Updates and Maintenance ............................128

How to Check for Software Updates...128

Steps to Check for Updates: ...............128

Installing System Updates and Security Patches ...............................129

Steps to Install Updates: .....................129

Understanding Pixel 9a's Update Schedule ...............................129

Clearing Cache and Optimizing System Performance ...............................130

Factory Reset Instructions and When to Do It...............................130

Keeping Apps Up to Date ....................130

Steps to Update Apps: ..........................131

Syncing Google Contacts, Calendar, and Gmail ...............................132

Steps to Sync: ...............................132

Using Google Maps for Navigation and Location Sharing ...............................133

Steps to Use Google Maps: ..................133

Accessing Google Drive and Google Docs....................................... 133

Steps to Use Google Drive:.................. 133

Setting Up Google Pay and Managing Payment Methods ............................... 134

Steps to Set Up Google Pay: ................ 134

Using Google Home App for Smart Home Control ....................................... 134

Steps to Use Google Home:................. 134

Exploring Google Stadia for Gaming.. 135

Steps to Use Google Stadia:................. 135

# Google Pixel 9a User Guide: The Complete Manual to Master Your Device**

Welcome to the **Google Pixel 9a User Guide**—your ultimate companion for unlocking the full potential of your smartphone! Whether you're a first-time Google Pixel 9a user or a seasoned Google enthusiast, this guide is designed to help you navigate every feature, setting, and hidden trick your device has to offer.

The **Google Pixel 9a** is packed with powerful performance, an impressive display, and a versatile camera system—all at an affordable price. But to truly make the most of your phone, you need to understand its capabilities. This book provides step-by-step instructions, practical tips, and expert advice on:

- ❖ **Getting Started:** Set up your device, transfer data, and personalize your home screen.
- ❖ **Mastering the Camera:** Learn pro tips for stunning photos and videos with the 9a's multi-lens setup.
- ❖ **Maximizing Battery Life:** Discover battery-saving techniques and fast-charging best practices.
- ❖ **Security & Privacy:** Set up fingerprint and face recognition, secure your data, and manage app permissions.
- ❖ **Hidden Features & Shortcuts:** Unlock secret tricks to boost productivity and enhance your user experience.
- ❖ **Troubleshooting & Maintenance:** Fix common issues, optimize performance, and keep your phone running smoothly.

With clear explanations, helpful screenshots, and easy-to-follow instructions, this guide ensures you'll become a **Google Pixel 9a expert** in no time.

Ready to explore everything your phone can do? Let's get started!

❖ **Your Google Pixel 9a journey begins here.**

# Chapter 1: Introduction to Your Google Pixel 9a

## Overview of the Google Pixel 9a

The Google Pixel 9a is a smartphone designed by Google that combines powerful features, smooth performance, and easy access to Google's services. Whether you're a first-time smartphone user or switching from another brand, the Pixel 9a is easy to use and offers a clean Android experience. This phone is known for its great camera, fast software updates, and integration with Google's apps and services.

## Key Features and Specifications

Here's a quick look at what makes the Pixel 9a stand out:

- **Display**: A high-quality screen, perfect for watching videos, browsing the web, and playing games.

- **Camera**: Pixel phones are famous for their camera quality, and the Pixel 9a continues that tradition. It includes powerful features like Night Sight (for great photos in low light), Portrait Mode (for professional-looking selfies), and more.

- **Battery Life**: The Pixel 9a offers an all-day battery life, so you don't have to worry about constantly charging.

- **Performance**: With a fast processor, you can easily run apps, play games, and switch between tasks without lag.

- **Google Assistant**: Your personal assistant that can help you with tasks, control smart home devices, send messages, and much more – all by using your voice.

- **Security**: The Pixel 9a includes a fingerprint sensor and other security features like facial recognition to keep your phone and data safe.

- **Software**: As a Google device, it gets updates directly from Google, so you'll always have the latest version of Android with the newest features and security patches.

- **Storage**: Enough storage to keep your apps, photos, videos, and other files. It also integrates with Google services like Google Drive, so you can store files online if you need more space.

## What's in the Box?

When you open the box for the Google Pixel 9a, you'll find the following items:

1. **Google Pixel 9a** – The main phone itself.

2. **USB-C Cable** – Used for charging the phone and connecting to other devices.

3. **Power Adapter** – A plug for charging the Pixel 9a.

4. **SIM Ejector Tool** – A small tool to open the SIM card tray.

5. **Quick Start Guide** – A simple guide to help you get started with your phone.

6. **Warranty Information** – Details on your phone's warranty, in case you need repairs or help with your device.

Note: The Google Pixel 9a may not come with accessories like headphones or a microSD card. You might need to buy some of these separately if you want them.

# Getting Started with Your Pixel 9a

Now that you know what's inside the box, here's how you can get started with your Google Pixel 9a:

## Insert the SIM Card:

- Use the SIM ejector tool to open the SIM card tray and insert your SIM card. This is how your phone connects to the mobile network.

## Power On Your Phone:

- Press and hold the power button on the side of the phone until the Google logo appears on the screen. Your phone will start up and show the welcome screen.

**Set Up Your Phone:**

- **Select your language**: Choose the language you want to use on your device.

- **Connect to Wi-Fi**: Connect to a Wi-Fi network to use the internet and download apps and updates.

- **Sign in to your Google Account**: If you already have a Google account (like Gmail or YouTube), sign in now to sync your apps, contacts, and photos.

- **Set up a screen lock**: For added security, you'll be asked to set up a PIN, password, or pattern. You can also set up fingerprint recognition or facial unlock later.

**Finish the Setup:**

- o After signing in and setting up security, your phone will guide you through some additional steps like transferring data from an old phone, setting up Google Assistant, and personalizing your settings.

Once you've completed these steps, you're ready to start using your Google Pixel 9a! You can start by exploring your home screen, downloading apps from the Google Play Store, or taking your first photo with the camera.

That's all for Chapter 1! You now have a basic understanding of your Google Pixel 9a and are ready to start using it. In the next chapters, we'll dive deeper into the features and functions of your new device.

# Chapter 2: Setting Up Your Google Pixel 9a

Congratulations on getting your new Google Pixel 9a! Now, let's go through the steps to get your device up and running. In this chapter, we'll cover everything from inserting your SIM card to transferring data from your old device and setting up your Google services.

## Inserting the SIM Card and microSD (if applicable)

Before you can start using your Google Pixel 9a, you'll need to insert a SIM card. The SIM card allows your phone to connect to the mobile network, make calls, and use data. Some phones also support a microSD card, which gives you extra storage for photos, videos, and apps. Here's how to do it:

## Inserting the SIM Card:

1. **Find the SIM tray**: On the side of the Pixel 9a, you'll see a small hole next to the SIM card tray.

2. **Use the SIM ejector tool**: Take the SIM ejector tool (it's included in the box) and gently insert it into the hole. This will pop the SIM tray out of the phone.

3. **Insert your SIM card**: Place your SIM card into the tray. Be sure to align the card properly so it fits snugly.

4. **Reinsert the tray**: Gently push the tray back into the phone until it's secure.

**Note**: If your Pixel 9a has a microSD slot, you can also insert a microSD card in the same tray to expand your storage. Make sure it's inserted in the correct orientation.

## Powering On Your Pixel 9a

Now that your SIM card is in place, let's power on your Pixel 9a.

1. **Press and hold the power button**: Find the power button on the side of your phone and press and hold it for a few seconds.

2. **Wait for the Google logo**: After a few moments, you'll see the Google logo appear on the screen, which means the phone is starting up.

**Tip**: If your phone doesn't turn on, make sure the battery is charged. If it's not, plug it in using the included charging cable and adapter, then try turning it on again.

## Initial Setup Guide

When your Pixel 9a turns on for the first time, it will guide you through a few initial setup steps. Here's what to expect:

## 1. Select your Language:

- The first thing you'll be asked to do is select the language you want to use on your device. You can choose from a wide variety of languages, so pick the one you're most comfortable with.

## 2. Connect to Wi-Fi:

- After selecting your language, you'll need to connect to a Wi-Fi network. This will allow you to download updates, apps, and anything else you need during setup.

  - Simply choose your Wi-Fi network from the list and enter your Wi-Fi password.

  - If you don't have a Wi-Fi connection, you can skip this step, but you will need Wi-Fi later to download apps and updates.

### 3. Sign in to Your Google Account:

- Next, you'll be prompted to sign in to your Google account. If you have a Gmail account or any other Google services (like YouTube, Google Photos, etc.), this is where you'll log in.

    o If you already have a Google account, enter your email address and password to sign in.

    o If you don't have a Google account yet, you can create one during this process. Simply follow the instructions to create a new account.

### Why is signing in to your Google account important?

- Signing in allows you to access Google services like Gmail, Google Play Store, Google Photos, and more.

- It also helps back up your data (photos, contacts, app settings) so you can easily restore it if you need to reset your phone or get a new one.

## Transferring Data from Your Old Device

If you're upgrading from another phone, you'll want to transfer your contacts, messages, apps, and other important data to your new Pixel 9a. Fortunately, Google makes this easy with its "**Switch to Android**" feature. Here's how to do it:

## Option 1: Using a Cable (Recommended for Fast Transfer)

1. **Connect both phones**: Using a USB-C to USB-C cable (or the included adapter if your old phone uses a different connector), connect your old phone to the Pixel 9a.

2. **Follow the prompts**: Your Pixel 9a will guide you through the process,

asking you what you want to transfer (contacts, apps, messages, photos, etc.).

3. **Complete the transfer**: Once the transfer is done, your data will be available on your new Pixel 9a.

## Option 2: Using Google Backup (No Cable Needed)

1. **Back up data on your old device**: Make sure your old phone is backed up to Google's cloud service (Google Drive). Most Android phones will automatically back up your data, including apps, contacts, and photos.

2. **Restore on your Pixel 9a**: During the setup process, when you sign in to your Google account, the Pixel 9a will offer to restore your data from the cloud backup. Just follow the instructions, and your old data will be transferred to your new device.

**Tip**: You can also use the **Google Photos app** to transfer your pictures and videos if you've been using it to back them up on your old device.

## Setting Up Google Services

After completing the initial setup and transferring your data, you'll be prompted to set up some of Google's services on your Pixel 9a. These services will make your phone more useful and secure.

**1. Google Assistant:**

- Google Assistant is a voice-controlled AI that helps you with tasks like sending messages, setting reminders, checking the weather, and much more.

- You can activate it by saying "Hey Google" or pressing and holding the home button.

- Follow the on-screen instructions to set up Google Assistant on your Pixel

9a. You might be asked to teach it your voice so it can recognize your commands.

## 2. Google Pay:

- If you want to use your Pixel 9a for contactless payments, you'll need to set up **Google Pay**. You can link your credit or debit cards to the Google Pay app, and then you can pay at stores that support NFC payments with just a tap of your phone.

- Open the **Google Pay** app from the Google Play Store and follow the instructions to set up your payment methods.

## 3. Google Cloud Backup:

- Google offers **cloud backup** for your apps, contacts, and data. To ensure your data is always backed up and accessible, turn on Google's backup feature. This way, if you ever lose or reset your phone, you can restore everything from the cloud.

- Go to **Settings** > **System** > **Backup** to make sure Google Backup is turned on.

That's all for Chapter 2! You've now successfully set up your Google Pixel 9a. You're connected to Wi-Fi, signed in to your Google account, transferred your data, and set up key Google services. In the next chapters, we'll explore how to get the most out of your phone, including using apps, customizing settings, and managing your security.

# Chapter 3: Navigating the Google Pixel 9a

Welcome to Chapter 3! Now that your Google Pixel 9a is set up, let's dive into navigating your phone. In this chapter, we'll cover how to interact with the home screen, use gestures for navigation, understand the status bar, customize your home screen, and manage notifications and widgets. By the end of this chapter, you'll be comfortable using your phone and adjusting it to your preferences.

## Understanding the Home Screen and Its Layout

The **Home Screen** is the main screen of your Google Pixel 9a, where you can access all of your apps, settings, and features. Here's a breakdown of what you'll find on the home screen:

## Key Components:

1. **App Icons**: These are the icons for the apps you use the most, like Phone, Messages, and Camera. You can add or remove these to organize your home screen.

2. **Search Bar**: At the top of the screen, you'll see a search bar that lets you quickly search the web or find apps, contacts, or settings.

3. **Dock**: At the bottom of your screen, there is a "dock" where you can place your favorite apps, like Phone, Messages, and Chrome. These apps will always be easy to access no matter which screen you're on.

4. **Home Screen Pages**: Your home screen isn't just one page; it's made up of several pages. You can swipe left or right to see more pages, and you can

also have multiple home screens for different app organization.

5. **App Drawer**: The App Drawer is where all your installed apps are stored. To access it, swipe up from the bottom of the screen. It's like a storage space for all your apps, not just the ones on your home screen.

## Navigating Using Gestures

The Pixel 9a uses **gesture navigation** instead of physical buttons for easier navigation. Here's how you can use gestures to move around your phone:

## Basic Gestures:

## Go to the Home Screen:

- **Swipe up** from the bottom of the screen. This takes you back to your home screen no matter where you are in the phone.

## Switch Between Apps:

- **Swipe up and hold**. This will show you the apps you've used recently, allowing you to switch between them easily. You can tap any app to open it or swipe up on an app to close it.

## Go Back:

- **Swipe from the left or right edge** of the screen. This will take you back to the previous screen or page.

## Open Google Assistant:

- **Swipe from the bottom corner**. This gesture opens Google Assistant, where you can give voice commands like "Set a timer" or "Play music."

**Tip**: If you prefer to use traditional navigation buttons (Back, Home, Recent), you can change your settings. Go to

**Settings** > **System** > **Gestures** and select "3-button navigation."

## Using the Status Bar and Quick Settings

The **Status Bar** and **Quick Settings** are key elements for managing your phone's settings and notifications.

**Status Bar:**

At the top of your screen, you'll see the **Status Bar**. This bar shows important information about your device, such as:

- **Wi-Fi Signal**: Shows if you are connected to Wi-Fi and the strength of the signal.

- **Battery Icon**: Displays your current battery level.

- **Mobile Signal**: Indicates if your phone is connected to a mobile network and how strong the signal is.

- **Time**: Shows the current time.

- **Notifications**: Alerts for things like messages, emails, or app updates. If you see an icon in the status bar, it means there's a notification waiting for you.

## Quick Settings:

To access **Quick Settings**, swipe **down** from the top of your screen. This will reveal a panel with toggles for various settings like:

- **Wi-Fi**: Turn your Wi-Fi on or off.

- **Bluetooth**: Quickly connect to Bluetooth devices like headphones or speakers.

- **Do Not Disturb**: Turn off notifications temporarily to avoid interruptions.

- **Brightness**: Adjust your screen's brightness level.

- **Airplane Mode**: Disable mobile network, Wi-Fi, and Bluetooth when you need to save battery or when flying.

You can tap any of these icons to turn features on or off. If you swipe down again, you'll see additional settings such as **Battery Saver**, **Location**, and **Mobile Hotspot**.

**Tip**: You can **customize Quick Settings** by tapping the pencil icon in the bottom left corner. This allows you to rearrange icons for easier access.

## Customizing Your Home Screen

Now that you know how to navigate around your Pixel 9a, let's personalize your home screen to make it truly yours. You can change things like your wallpaper, organize apps, and add shortcuts for quick access.

## 1. Change Your Wallpaper:

To change the wallpaper (the background image on your home screen):

1. **Long press** on any empty space on the home screen.

2. Tap **Wallpaper & Style**.

3. You can choose from a selection of **wallpaper categories**, including static and live wallpapers, or upload your own photo.

4. Select your preferred wallpaper and tap **Set Wallpaper**.

## 2. Move or Remove Apps:

To organize your home screen, you can move or remove apps as follows:

1. **Move an app**: Tap and hold the app icon you want to move. Drag it to a new spot on the home screen.

2. **Remove an app**: Tap and hold the app icon. If you want to remove it

from the home screen but keep it on the device, drag it to the "Remove" area at the top of the screen. If you want to uninstall it, drag it to **Uninstall**.

### 3. Create Folders:

You can create folders to group similar apps together. To create a folder:

1. Tap and hold an app icon.

2. Drag it over another app you want to group it with. A folder will automatically be created.

3. You can name the folder and add more apps by dragging them into it.

### 4. Add Widgets:

Widgets allow you to see information from apps directly on your home screen without opening them. Here's how to add one:

1. **Long press** on an empty space on your home screen.

2. Tap **Widgets**.

3. Browse through the available widgets and tap on one you want to add.

4. Select the size and location on your home screen where you want the widget to appear.

**Examples of useful widgets**: Weather, Calendar, Music player, Google Assistant, News updates.

## Managing Notifications and Widgets

Notifications help you stay updated with important information, while widgets give you quick access to key data or actions.

## Managing Notifications:

When you receive a notification, it appears in the **Status Bar** at the top of your screen. Here's how to manage them:

1. **View notifications**: Swipe **down** from the top of your screen to open

the notification shade and see your alerts.

2. **Clear notifications**: To remove a notification, swipe it to the side. If you want to clear all notifications, tap **Clear All**.

3. **Manage notifications**: You can control how apps notify you by going to **Settings** > **Apps & Notifications** > **Notifications**. From here, you can customize how notifications appear for each app, like turning off sound or vibration.

**Tip**: If you swipe a notification to the left or right, it will dismiss the notification. If you tap on it, it opens the related app.

That's it for Chapter 3! You've learned how to navigate the Google Pixel 9a, understand the home screen layout, use gestures, access the status bar and quick settings, and customize your home screen.

You're now ready to start using your phone to its full potential! In the next chapter, we'll explore how to connect to Wi-Fi, manage mobile networks, and set up Bluetooth and other connections.

# Chapter 4: Connecting to Wi-Fi and Mobile Networks

In this chapter, we will cover all the ways to connect your Google Pixel 9a to the internet and other networks, including Wi-Fi, mobile data, Bluetooth, and VPNs. You'll also learn how to manage settings for these connections and how to use Airplane mode when needed.

## Connecting to Wi-Fi Networks

Wi-Fi is one of the most common ways to connect to the internet, and it's typically faster and more reliable than using mobile data. Here's how to connect your Pixel 9a to a Wi-Fi network:

### Steps to Connect to Wi-Fi:
1. **Open Quick Settings**:

    o Swipe down from the top of the screen to open the **Quick Settings** panel.

2. **Turn on Wi-Fi**:

   o If Wi-Fi is off, tap the **Wi-Fi icon** to turn it on. The icon will turn blue or white when it's enabled.

3. **Choose a Network**:

   o After turning on Wi-Fi, your phone will automatically scan for available networks. Tap on the **Wi-Fi network** you want to connect to.

4. **Enter the Password**:

   o If the network is secured, you'll be prompted to enter the **Wi-Fi password**. Type it in and tap **Connect**.

5. **Confirm Connection**:

   o Once connected, the Wi-Fi icon in the status bar will show the signal strength, confirming you're connected to the internet.

**Tip**: If you often connect to the same Wi-Fi networks (home, work, etc.), your phone will automatically reconnect to these networks when they are in range.

## Managing Wi-Fi Settings

Your Pixel 9a offers various options to manage your Wi-Fi connections, such as configuring advanced settings, managing saved networks, and ensuring your phone connects securely.

### Advanced Wi-Fi Settings:

1. **Access Wi-Fi Settings**:

   o Go to **Settings** > **Network & Internet** > **Wi-Fi**. This will show you all available networks.

2. **Save Networks**:

   ○ When you connect to a network, your phone will automatically save the connection for future use. You can view saved networks under **Saved networks** in the Wi-Fi settings.

3. **Toggle Wi-Fi Preferences**:

   ○ In **Wi-Fi preferences**, you can adjust settings like:

     ▪ **Wi-Fi assistant** (helps automatically switch to stronger Wi-Fi when available).

     ▪ **Keep Wi-Fi on during sleep** (allows your phone to stay connected to Wi-Fi even when it's not being actively used).

4. **Forget a Network**:

   o To remove a saved Wi-Fi network, tap the **network name**, then select **Forget**. This will stop your Pixel from connecting to that network automatically.

5. **Use Wi-Fi Calling**:

   o If you're in an area with poor mobile reception but good Wi-Fi, you can enable **Wi-Fi calling** to make and receive calls over Wi-Fi. Go to **Settings > Network & Internet > Wi-Fi calling**, and turn it on if available.

## Setting Up Mobile Data and Roaming

Mobile data allows you to use the internet on your phone when you're not connected to Wi-Fi. Roaming lets you use mobile data while you're traveling outside your carrier's coverage area.

## Enable Mobile Data:

1. **Turn on Mobile Data**:

   o Open **Quick Settings** by swiping down from the top of the screen.

   o Tap the **Mobile Data icon** to turn it on. The icon will turn blue or white when mobile data is enabled.

2. **Check Data Usage**:

   o To monitor your data usage, go to **Settings** > **Network & Internet** > **Mobile network** > **Data usage**. Here, you can set up data usage warnings or limits to avoid overages.

## Setting Up Roaming:

1. **Turn on Roaming**:

   o When traveling outside your carrier's coverage area, you'll need to enable **roaming** to use mobile data.

   o Go to **Settings** > **Network & Internet** > **Mobile network** > **Roaming**, and turn on **Data roaming** to allow roaming services.

**Important**: Keep in mind that roaming can result in additional charges, so it's a good idea to check with your carrier about roaming fees.

## Using Airplane Mode

Airplane Mode is a feature that turns off all wireless connections on your phone (Wi-Fi, mobile data, Bluetooth, etc.) at once. It's useful when you're traveling on an airplane, in certain public places, or when you need to conserve battery.

## Turning on Airplane Mode:
1. **Quick Settings**:

   o Swipe down from the top of your screen to open **Quick Settings**.

   o Tap the **Airplane Mode icon** to turn it on. When activated, all wireless connections (Wi-Fi, mobile data, Bluetooth) will be disabled.

2. **Turning Off Airplane Mode**:

   o To go back online, simply tap the **Airplane Mode icon** again in Quick Settings to turn it off.

**Tip**: You can manually enable Wi-Fi and Bluetooth while Airplane Mode is on by tapping the corresponding icons in Quick Settings. This way, you can still connect to

Wi-Fi or Bluetooth while keeping mobile data off.

## Connecting to Bluetooth Devices

Bluetooth lets you wirelessly connect your phone to devices like headphones, speakers, car systems, and more. Here's how to set it up:

## Connecting to Bluetooth:

1. **Turn on Bluetooth**:

   o Swipe down from the top of the screen to open **Quick Settings**.

   o Tap the **Bluetooth icon** to enable Bluetooth.

2. **Pairing a Bluetooth Device**:

   o Once Bluetooth is turned on, your Pixel 9a will scan for available devices.

   o Go to **Settings** > **Connected devices** > **Pair new device**.

- Your phone will list available devices. Tap on the name of the device you want to connect to (e.g., headphones or a speaker).

3. **Enter Pairing Code (if needed):**

- Some Bluetooth devices may ask for a pairing code. Follow the instructions on the device screen, then tap **Pair**.

4. **Disconnecting or Unpairing:**

- To disconnect a device, go to **Settings** > **Connected devices** and tap on the device name, then select **Disconnect**.

- To unpair a device completely, select **Forget**.

## Setting Up a VPN Connection

A VPN (Virtual Private Network) is a secure connection that helps protect your privacy when using the internet, especially when using public Wi-Fi networks.

**Setting Up a VPN:**

1. **Access VPN Settings:**

   ○ Go to **Settings** > **Network & Internet** > **VPN**.

2. **Add a VPN:**

   ○ Tap **Add VPN** and enter the necessary information (e.g., the VPN provider's details, username, and password). You can get these details from your VPN provider (either your employer or a third-party service).

3. **Connect to the VPN:**

   ○ Once the VPN is set up, you can tap on the VPN name to connect. Your phone will ask for your username and password if required.

4. **Disconnect from the VPN:**

   ○ To disconnect, go back to **Settings** > **Network & Internet** > **VPN** and tap **Disconnect**.

**Tip**: VPN connections may slow down your internet speed, so only use them when necessary, especially if you're on a slow connection.

That's all for Chapter 4! You now know how to connect your Pixel 9a to Wi-Fi, manage mobile data, set up roaming, use Airplane mode, pair with Bluetooth devices, and set up a VPN connection. In the next chapter, we'll dive into using the Pixel 9a's camera to capture stunning photos and videos!

# Chapter 5: Making Calls and Sending Messages

In this chapter, we'll cover how to make and receive calls, send text messages, use Google Assistant for hands-free calling, and manage your voicemail. Let's start with the basics of communication on your Google Pixel 9a.

## Making and Receiving Voice Calls

Making and receiving calls on the Google Pixel 9a is simple and intuitive. Here's how to make a call:

## Making a Call:

1. **Open the Phone app**: Tap on the **Phone app** icon (it looks like a green phone receiver) from your home screen or app drawer.

2. **Dial the Number**:

   o Use the **Keypad** to manually dial a number or tap the

**Contacts** tab to search for someone in your contacts list.

3. **Tap the Call Button**: After entering the number or selecting the contact, tap the **Call icon** (a green phone receiver) to start the call.

## Receiving a Call:

- When you receive a call, the incoming number or contact name will appear on your screen.

- To answer the call, swipe **up** or tap the **Answer button**.

- To decline a call, swipe **down** or tap the **Decline button**.

**Tip**: You can also use the **Speakerphone**, **Mute**, or **Hold** options during a call, which are displayed on the screen once the call is active.

## Managing Contacts and Favorites

Your contacts are where you store phone numbers, email addresses, and other details of the people you connect with regularly. Here's how you can manage them:

### Adding a New Contact:

1. Open the **Contacts app**.

2. Tap the **plus (+)** icon or **Create new contact**.

3. Enter the person's name, phone number, email address, and any other relevant details.

4. Tap **Save** when you're done.

### Marking Favorites:

To mark a contact as a favorite:

1. Open the **Contacts app**.

2. Find the contact you want to mark as a favorite.

3. Tap the **star icon** next to their name. A solid star means they're now a favorite.

Favorites are easily accessible, and you can quickly call or message them by going to the **Favorites tab** in the **Phone app**.

## Using Google Assistant for Hands-Free Calling

Google Assistant makes it easy to make calls without having to touch your phone. Here's how to use it for hands-free calling:

1. **Activate Google Assistant**:

   ○ Say "**Hey Google**" or press and hold the **Home button** to activate Google Assistant.

2. **Make the Call**:

   ○ Once Google Assistant is listening, simply say "**Call [contact name]**" or "**Dial [phone number]**".

3. **Google Assistant Will Make the Call**:

   ○ Google Assistant will automatically dial the number or contact you requested.

**Tip**: You can also ask Google Assistant to **send a text** or **check missed calls** while you're busy.

## Sending Text Messages via SMS, MMS, and RCS

The Google Pixel 9a allows you to send text messages in several formats: SMS (Short Message Service), MMS (Multimedia Messaging Service), and RCS (Rich Communication Services).

### Sending an SMS or MMS:

1. **Open the Messages app**.

2. Tap the **plus (+)** icon or **Start chat** to create a new message.

3. **Enter the recipient's phone number** or choose a contact from your list.

4. **Type your message** in the text field.

5. If you want to send an image or video (MMS), tap the **attachment icon** (a paperclip), select the media you want to send, and then tap **Send**.

## What's the Difference Between SMS, MMS, and RCS?

- **SMS**: Standard text messages (limited to text and small attachments like pictures).

- **MMS**: Multimedia messages that allow you to send pictures, videos, and audio files.

- **RCS**: Rich Communication Services (an upgraded messaging system with more features, like read receipts and typing indicators) that is supported by many Android devices, including your Pixel 9a.

**Note**: To use RCS, both you and the person you're messaging must have RCS-enabled devices and carriers that support it.

## Using Google Messages for Chat Features

Google Messages is the default messaging app on your Pixel 9a, and it supports chat features like RCS for richer messaging experiences. Here's how to enable and use chat features:

1. **Enable RCS**:

   o Open the **Messages app**.

   o Tap the three dots (menu icon) in the top-right corner.

   o Tap **Settings** > **Chat features**.

   o Enable **Enable chat features**. This allows you to send and receive messages over Wi-Fi or mobile data with features like typing indicators, read receipts, and high-quality media.

2. **Start a Chat with RCS**:

   ○ When you send a message to someone who also has RCS enabled, you'll see indicators like **"Typing..."** or **"Read by [contact name]"**.

   ○ You can send larger images, videos, and other media files without worrying about SMS/MMS limits.

## Setting Up Voicemail

Voicemail lets you receive voice messages when you miss a call. Here's how to set it up on your Google Pixel 9a:

1. **Open the Phone app**.

2. Tap the **three dots** in the top-right corner.

3. Tap **Settings** > **Voicemail**.

4. Follow the instructions to **set up your voicemail**. This will usually include recording a greeting and setting up a voicemail password.

**Accessing Voicemail:**

- To check your voicemail, open the **Phone app** and tap the **Voicemail** tab.

- You can listen to, delete, or save voicemail messages from this screen.

**Tip**: Some carriers allow you to access voicemail by holding down the **1 key** on the dial pad.

# Chapter 6: Using the Camera

In this chapter, we'll explore the powerful camera features of the Google Pixel 9a. Whether you're capturing photos, recording videos, or editing your images, the Pixel 9a's camera has everything you need to take amazing shots.

## Overview of the Pixel 9a's Camera Features

The Pixel 9a's camera offers a range of powerful features, including the ability to take stunning photos in different lighting conditions, create portrait shots, and more. Some key features include:

- **Night Sight**: Allows you to take clear photos in low-light environments.

- **Portrait Mode**: Creates a professional-looking blurred background (bokeh effect) around your subject.

- **Wide-Angle Lens**: Captures more of the scene, great for landscapes or group photos.

## Taking Photos with the Rear and Front Camera

To take a photo with the rear camera:

1. **Open the Camera app** (it's usually on your home screen).

2. **Point the camera** at your subject.

3. Tap the **shutter button** (the circle icon) to take a picture.

To switch to the front-facing camera (for selfies):

1. Tap the **camera switch icon** (it looks like a circular arrow) in the Camera app.

2. The front camera will activate, and you can take selfies just like you would with the rear camera.

## Using Night Sight, Portrait Mode, and Other Special Camera Modes
### Night Sight:

Night Sight helps you take clear, bright photos even in very low light. When you're in a low-light environment:

1. Open the **Camera app**.

2. Swipe left to access **Night Sight** mode.

3. Point the camera at your subject and hold still for a few seconds. The camera will automatically adjust to capture the best shot.

### Portrait Mode:
To take a portrait with a blurred background:

1. Open the **Camera app**.

2. Swipe to **Portrait** mode.

3. Frame your subject, and the camera will automatically apply the bokeh effect to create a professional-looking portrait.

## Other Camera Modes:

- **Panorama**: Great for wide landscape shots. Swipe to the **Panorama** mode and take a wide photo.

- **Video**: To record a video, swipe to the **Video** mode and press the record button.

## Recording Videos
To record videos:

1. Open the **Camera app**.

2. Swipe to **Video** mode.

3. Tap the **record button** to start recording, and tap it again to stop.

## Editing and Sharing Photos/Videos
After taking photos or videos, you can edit them right from the Photos app:

1. Open the **Photos app**.

2. Tap on a photo or video you want to edit.

3. Tap the **Edit icon** (looks like a pencil).

4. You can adjust things like brightness, contrast, and filters.

Once you're happy with your edits, tap **Share** to send your photo or video via email, text, or social media.

## Using Google Photos for Backups and Organization

Google Photos automatically backs up your photos and videos to the cloud, ensuring you never lose them. You can also organize and search your photos by date, location, or even by the people in them.

1. Open the **Google Photos app**.

2. Tap the **three dots** in the top-right corner to access settings.

3. Turn on **Backup & Sync** to automatically upload your photos to Google Drive.

That concludes Chapters 5 and 6! You now know how to make calls, send messages, use Google Assistant for hands-free communication, and take beautiful photos with your Google Pixel 9a. Next, we'll dive into using Google Assistant to control your phone and manage everyday tasks.

# Chapter 7: Using Google Assistant

Google Assistant is an AI-powered virtual assistant that helps you perform tasks using just your voice. It can make calls, send texts, set reminders, navigate, play music, and much more. Let's dive into how to set up and use Google Assistant on your Google Pixel 9a.

## What is Google Assistant?

Google Assistant is a smart assistant powered by Google's AI technology. It helps you complete tasks on your device with voice commands, saving you time and offering a hands-free experience. Google Assistant can:

- Send texts and make calls

- Play music and videos

- Get information (weather, sports, news)

- Control smart devices (if you have connected smart home devices)

- Navigate and get directions

- Set alarms, timers, and reminders

## Activating and Customizing Google Assistant

Google Assistant is pre-installed on your Pixel 9a, and it's easy to activate. Here's how to get started:

## Activating Google Assistant:

1. **Voice Activation**:

   o Simply say **"Hey Google"** or **"Ok Google"** to activate the Assistant.

2. **Button Activation**:

   o Press and hold the **Home button** on your Pixel 9a to activate Google Assistant.

**Tip**: Make sure "Google Assistant" is turned on in your settings if it's not responding. Go to **Settings** > **Google** > **Search, Assistant & Voice** > **Google Assistant**, and make sure it's enabled.

## Customizing Google Assistant:

1. **Personalize Google Assistant**:

   o Go to **Settings** > **Google** > **Search, Assistant & Voice** > **Google Assistant**.

   o Here, you can change settings like the Assistant's voice, language, and personalized recommendations.

2. **Voice Match**:

   o Google Assistant uses **Voice Match** to recognize your voice and give personalized responses. Under the **Google Assistant** settings, tap **Voice**

**Match** to train it to recognize your voice.

3. **Linking Accounts:**

   o You can link your Google account, smart home devices, and other services (like Spotify or YouTube) to make your Assistant smarter.

## Using Voice Commands to Control Your Device

Once Google Assistant is set up, you can use voice commands to control many functions on your phone. Here are a few common commands:

### Make Calls:

- Say, **"Hey Google, call [contact name]"** to dial someone.

- Example: "Hey Google, call Mom."

**Send Text Messages:**

- Say, **"Hey Google, send a text to [contact name]"**, then dictate your message.

- Example: "Hey Google, send a text to John saying 'I'll be there in 10 minutes.'"

**Control Music and Media:**

- Say, **"Hey Google, play some music"** or **"Hey Google, play [song/artist]"**.

- You can also control volume, pause, skip songs, and more.

**Set Reminders and Alarms:**

- Say, **"Hey Google, set a reminder to buy groceries at 3 PM"**.

- Example: "Hey Google, set an alarm for 7 AM."

**Get Directions:**

- Say, "**Hey Google, navigate to [destination]**" to get directions in Google Maps.

## Integrating Google Assistant with Other Apps

Google Assistant works with many third-party apps to make your phone smarter. You can integrate apps such as music services, smart home devices, and more.

**Connecting Smart Home Devices:**

1. Open the **Google Home app**.

2. Tap the + icon to add a device.

3. Follow the instructions to connect your smart lights, thermostat, and other compatible devices.

4. Once connected, you can use Google Assistant to control them with commands like:

- o "Hey Google, turn off the lights."

- o "Hey Google, set the temperature to 72 degrees."

## Third-Party App Integration:

Google Assistant can integrate with apps like Spotify, YouTube, and WhatsApp. To connect apps:

1. Open the **Google Assistant settings** (Settings > Google > Search, Assistant & Voice > Google Assistant).

2. Scroll to **Services** and select the app you want to connect.

3. Follow the steps to link the app to Google Assistant.

## Creating Routines for Everyday Tasks

Google Assistant allows you to automate multiple actions with a single command by creating routines. This is great for everyday tasks like turning off lights and setting alarms, or getting weather updates when you wake up.

**Setting Up a Routine:**

1. Open **Google Assistant** by saying, "**Hey Google**".

2. Tap on the **Profile icon** and go to **Routines**.

3. Tap the + button to create a new routine.

4. Add actions such as:

   o **Turn on/off lights**

   o **Read the news**

   o **Play music**

   o **Set a reminder**

   o **Get the weather**

5. Customize the routine by selecting a specific time or phrase to activate it (e.g., "Good morning" to start your morning routine).

6. Save your routine.

## Example of a Morning Routine:

- When you say, **"Hey Google, good morning,"** Google Assistant could:

    o Turn on the lights.

    o Tell you the weather.

    o Play your favorite playlist.

    o Read your calendar events for the day.

## Using Google Assistant for Hands-Free Navigation

Google Assistant is perfect for navigating when you're driving or walking and need to keep your hands free. Here's how to use it for hands-free navigation:

## Getting Directions:

- Simply say, "**Hey Google, navigate to [destination]**".

- Google Assistant will open Google Maps and start giving you turn-by-turn directions.

## Control Navigation During the Trip:

- You can also use voice commands during your trip:

  o "**Hey Google, what's my ETA?**" to check the estimated time of arrival.

  o "**Hey Google, reroute**" to find an alternate route.

  o "**Hey Google, stop navigation**" to stop the directions.

# Chapter 8: Setting Up and Using Apps

In this chapter, we'll explore how to download, manage, and organize apps on your Google Pixel 9a, as well as how to manage app permissions and subscriptions.

## Downloading Apps from Google Play Store

The **Google Play Store** is where you can find thousands of apps, games, and media to download to your Pixel 9a. Here's how to download an app:

## Steps to Download an App:

1. Open the **Google Play Store** by tapping the Play Store icon.

2. Tap the **search bar** at the top and type the name of the app you want to download.

3. Select the app from the search results.

4. Tap the **Install** button to start downloading the app.

5. Once the app is installed, you can tap **Open** to launch it.

**Tip**: To install apps on multiple devices linked to your Google account, you can do so directly from the Google Play website.

## Managing Installed Apps

Once you've downloaded apps, you can easily manage them. Here's how:

## Viewing Installed Apps:

1. Open the **App Drawer** by swiping up on the home screen.

2. Scroll through the list of apps or use the **search bar** at the top to find a specific app.

## Updating Apps:

1. Open the **Google Play Store**.

2. Tap on the **Menu** icon (three horizontal lines) in the top-left corner and go to **My apps & games**.

3. You'll see a list of apps that need updates. Tap **Update All** to update all apps or select individual apps to update.

## Checking App Details:

1. In the **Play Store**, go to **My apps & games**.

2. Tap on any app to see more details like version, size, and permissions.

## Using Google Play Services and Subscriptions

Google Play offers services and subscriptions, such as music, movies, and cloud storage. Here's how to use them:

## Managing Subscriptions:

1. Open the **Google Play Store**.

2. Tap the **Menu** icon and select **Subscriptions**.

3. Here you can view and manage active subscriptions, like Google Play Music, YouTube Premium, and more.

**Google Play Services:**
Google Play Services runs in the background to keep your apps updated and help manage features like authentication and synchronization with Google services.

**Tip**: Make sure **Google Play Services** is updated to ensure that apps work properly.

**Organizing Apps into Folders**
Organizing apps into folders can help keep your home screen tidy and make apps easier to access.

**Creating an App Folder:**
1. Tap and hold on an app icon.

2. Drag it on top of another app you want in the same folder.

3. A folder will be created, and you can rename it by tapping the **folder name**.

## Adding More Apps to a Folder:

- Simply drag more apps into the existing folder.

## Managing App Permissions

Your Pixel 9a allows you to control what information apps can access, like your location, camera, or contacts. Here's how to manage app permissions:

## Granting or Revoking Permissions:

1. Go to **Settings** > **Apps** > [**App Name**].

2. Tap **Permissions** to see what the app has access to.

3. Toggle permissions on or off as needed.

**Tip**: For privacy, only grant apps permissions that are necessary for their function.

## Uninstalling Apps
If you no longer need an app, you can easily uninstall it to free up space:

## Steps to Uninstall an App:
1. Open the **App Drawer**.

2. Tap and hold the app you want to uninstall.

3. Select **Uninstall** from the options.

4. Confirm by tapping **OK**.

# Chapter 9: Managing Battery Life

In this chapter, we will go over how to manage your Pixel 9a's battery life, check battery health, and use features that help extend its battery life.

## Checking Battery Status and Health

To monitor the battery status and health of your Pixel 9a:

1. Go to **Settings** > **Battery**.

2. Here, you'll see the battery usage for the day and information about your battery's health (e.g., charging cycles and overall lifespan).

## Power-Saving Modes and Settings

Power-saving features can help extend battery life, especially when you're running low on charge.

**Enabling Power Saver:**

1. Go to **Settings** > **Battery** > **Battery Saver**.

2. Toggle **Battery Saver** on to limit background processes and extend battery life.

**Tips to Extend Battery Life**

1. **Lower Screen Brightness**: Use **Adaptive Brightness** or manually lower the brightness.

2. **Limit Background Apps**: Close unused apps that consume battery in the background.

3. **Turn off Unused Features**: Disable Wi-Fi, Bluetooth, or GPS when not in use.

4. **Use Dark Mode**: Dark Mode can save battery on OLED displays.

**Charging Your Google Pixel 9a (Wired and Wireless)**

To charge your Pixel 9a:

## Wired Charging:

1. Plug the **USB-C charging cable** into your Pixel 9a and the other end into a charger.

2. Your phone will begin charging immediately.

## Wireless Charging:

- If you have a **wireless charging pad**, place your phone on the pad to charge without cables.

## Using Battery Optimization Features

Battery optimization can reduce battery consumption by limiting background apps:

1. Go to **Settings** > **Battery** > **Battery optimization**.

2. Tap **Optimize** next to individual apps to limit their background activity.

## Understanding Fast Charging and Adaptive Charging
### Fast Charging:

- Your Pixel 9a supports **fast charging**, which charges your phone quickly when plugged into a compatible charger.

### Adaptive Charging:

- **Adaptive Charging** optimizes the charging speed to protect the battery and extend its lifespan, especially when charging overnight.

With this information, you now have a thorough understanding of managing your battery, using apps, and taking full advantage of Google Assistant on your Google Pixel 9a!

# Chapter 10: Data and Security

Your Google Pixel 9a comes equipped with multiple features to help you secure your device and protect your data. In this chapter, we will walk through the essential security settings and best practices to keep your information safe.

## Setting Up a Secure Lock Screen (PIN, Pattern, Password)

To keep your phone secure, it's important to set up a lock screen using a PIN, pattern, or password.

## Steps to Set Up a Lock Screen:

1. Go to **Settings** > **Security** > **Screen lock**.

2. Choose from the available options: **Pattern**, **PIN**, or **Password**.

3. Follow the on-screen prompts to set up your preferred method of unlocking your phone.

**Tip**: For the highest level of security, we recommend using a strong password, especially if your phone contains sensitive information.

## Using Fingerprint and Facial Recognition for Security

In addition to traditional lock screens, you can use **Fingerprint** and **Facial Recognition** to unlock your Pixel 9a more quickly and securely.

### Setting Up Fingerprint Unlock:

1. Go to **Settings** > **Security** > **Fingerprint**.

2. Follow the prompts to register your fingerprint by placing your finger on the sensor multiple times.

3. Once set up, you can unlock your phone simply by placing your finger on the fingerprint sensor.

## Setting Up Face Unlock:

1. Go to **Settings** > **Security** > **Face unlock**.

2. Follow the prompts to scan your face for recognition.

3. After setup, you can unlock your phone by simply looking at it.

**Note**: Both fingerprint and face unlock provide a faster way to access your device, but keep in mind that face unlock may be less secure than a PIN, pattern, or password.

## Setting Up Google Find My Device

Google's **Find My Device** helps you locate, lock, or erase your Pixel 9a if it's lost or stolen.

## Steps to Set Up Find My Device:

1. Go to **Settings** > **Security** > **Find My Device**.

2. Make sure it is turned on. You may need to sign in to your Google account if you haven't already.

3. If your phone is lost, you can visit the **Find My Device** website (or use the app on another device) to locate your phone on a map, lock it remotely, or erase all data if necessary.

## Managing App Permissions and Privacy Settings

Your Pixel 9a lets you control what information apps can access. This includes things like your location, contacts, and camera.

## Steps to Manage App Permissions:

1. Go to **Settings** > **Privacy** > **Permission manager**.

2. You can see and control what each app can access, like your camera, location, or microphone. Tap on an app to adjust its permissions.

**Tip**: Be selective about granting permissions to apps. Only allow access to what is necessary for the app to function.

## Backing Up and Restoring Your Data

Backing up your data ensures you won't lose important information, such as photos, contacts, or app data.

### Steps to Backup Your Data:

1. Go to **Settings** > **Google** > **Backup**.

2. Toggle on **Back up to Google Drive** to automatically back up data such as apps, call history, contacts, photos, and videos.

### Steps to Restore Your Data:

• When setting up a new Pixel device or after a factory reset, you can restore your data from a previous backup during the initial setup process. Simply sign into your Google account, and your backed-up data will be restored.

## Using Two-Factor Authentication for Google Services

Two-factor authentication (2FA) adds an extra layer of security to your Google account. It requires both your password and a second verification step to log in.

## Steps to Enable Two-Factor Authentication:

1. Open the **Google Play Store** or **Google Settings** on your Pixel 9a.

2. Go to **Security** > **2-Step Verification**.

3. Follow the instructions to enable 2FA using methods like text message, Google Authenticator, or a physical security key.

**Tip**: With 2FA enabled, even if someone gets your password, they won't be able to access your account without the second factor of authentication.

# Chapter 11: Managing Storage and Files

Managing your device's storage and files is essential for ensuring smooth performance and ample space for new content. Let's dive into how you can check your storage, move files, and manage apps.

## Checking Available Storage on Your Pixel 9a

To check how much storage is left on your device:

1. Go to **Settings** > **Storage**.

2. Here, you'll see an overview of your available space and how much storage is being used by apps, photos, videos, and other files.

**Tip**: If your storage is nearly full, you can use the **Free up space** feature to delete files or apps that you no longer need.

## Moving Files Between Internal Storage and SD Card (if applicable)

If your Pixel 9a supports SD cards, you can move files between the internal storage and the SD card to free up space.

### Steps to Move Files:

1. Open the **Files app**.

2. Select the file you want to move (e.g., a photo or document).

3. Tap the **three dots** in the top-right corner and select **Move to**.

4. Choose your SD card as the destination and move the file.

## Using Google Drive for Cloud Storage

Google Drive provides 15 GB of free cloud storage, and you can use it to back up important files, photos, and documents.

## Steps to Upload Files to Google Drive:

1. Open the **Google Drive app**.

2. Tap the + icon to upload a file.

3. Select **Upload** and choose the file you want to upload from your device.

## Managing Files with the Files App

The **Files app** helps you organize, search, and manage your files.

## Features of the Files App:

- **Browse files**: Easily view all your files stored on your device.

- **Search**: Quickly search for specific files.

- **Clean up**: The app provides suggestions to clean up unnecessary files, such as cached data or duplicate photos.

## Deleting Files and Managing Space

To free up storage, you may want to delete files that are no longer needed.

### Steps to Delete Files:

1. Open the **Files app**.

2. Select the file you wish to delete.

3. Tap the **trash can** icon to delete the file.

4. To free up space, you can also clear cached data by going to **Settings > Storage > Cache data**.

## Using Google Photos for Photo and Video Storage

Google Photos automatically backs up your photos and videos to the cloud, keeping them safe and accessible on any device.

### Steps to Backup Photos:

1. Open the **Google Photos app**.

2. Tap the **Menu** icon (three lines) and go to **Settings > Backup & sync**.

3. Toggle **Backup & sync** to automatically back up your photos and videos.

# Chapter 12: Customizing Your Google Pixel 9a

Personalizing your Google Pixel 9a will make it truly yours. From changing the wallpaper to adjusting system settings, you can customize nearly every aspect of your phone.

## Changing the Wallpaper and Themes

You can change the wallpaper on your home screen, lock screen, or both. You can also apply themes for a unique look.

## Steps to Change Wallpaper:

1. Tap and hold on the **home screen**.

2. Select **Wallpaper & style**.

3. Choose from default wallpapers, your own photos, or themes that change the look of your phone.

## Customizing the Lock Screen and Home Screen Settings

You can customize your Pixel 9a's lock screen and home screen with widgets, app icons, and shortcuts.

### To Customize the Home Screen:

1. Tap and hold on the home screen.

2. Choose **Home settings** to adjust things like icon size, grid layout, and app icons.

3. Add widgets by holding down an empty spot on the home screen, then selecting **Widgets**.

## Adjusting System Font, Display, and Animation Speed

You can adjust the font size, screen display, and even the speed of animations for a smoother experience.

### Steps to Adjust Display:

1. Go to **Settings** > **Display** > **Font size**.

2. Choose the font size that suits you best.

3. Adjust the **Animation scale** by going to **Developer options** (tap 7 times on **Build number** in **Settings > About phone**).

## Setting Up Dark Mode and Other Display Settings

Dark mode reduces eye strain and saves battery life on OLED displays. You can enable it across your entire system or just in specific apps.

### Steps to Enable Dark Mode:

1. Go to **Settings > Display > Dark theme**.

2. Toggle it on for a system-wide dark mode.

**Tip**: You can also schedule dark mode to turn on automatically at sunset or at a specific time.

## Sound and Notification Settings

Customizing your phone's sound and notification settings helps personalize alerts for different apps, ringtones, and system notifications.

### Adjusting Sound Settings:
1. Go to **Settings** > **Sound**.

2. From here, you can adjust **volume levels**, set different **ringtones** for calls, notifications, and alarms, and manage **Do Not Disturb** settings.

## Creating Custom Shortcuts for Apps

To make accessing apps easier, you can create custom shortcuts on your home screen.

### Steps to Create a Shortcut:
1. Tap and hold on an app in the app drawer.

2. Select **Add shortcut** or drag the app to the home screen.

# Chapter 13: Advanced Features

The Pixel 9a has some advanced features to help you get the most out of your device. From smart home control to digital wellbeing, these features will enhance your experience.

## Using the Google Pixel 9a with a Smart Home Setup

If you have smart home devices, such as lights, thermostats, or security cameras, you can control them through your Pixel 9a using Google Assistant.

## Setting Up Digital Wellbeing and Focus Mode

Digital Wellbeing helps you manage your phone usage by tracking screen time, setting app limits, and creating distraction-free environments with Focus Mode.

**Steps to Set Up Focus Mode:**

1. Go to **Settings** > **Digital Wellbeing & parental controls.**

2. Tap on **Focus Mode** and select which apps to silence while you need focus time.

## Managing Screen Time and App Limits

Track your screen time and set limits for specific apps to help manage your device use.

## Setting Up Gesture Navigation and Customizing It

Pixel 9a supports gesture navigation, which allows you to swipe and navigate without using buttons.

## Using Google Lens for Visual Search

Google Lens allows you to search for objects or text by pointing your camera at them.

## Exploring the Pixel 9a's "Now Playing" Feature

The **Now Playing** feature automatically identifies songs playing in your surroundings.

That concludes Chapter 13. Stay tuned for the rest of the manual to maximize your Pixel 9a's potential!

# Chapter 14: Connectivity with Other Devices

Your Google Pixel 9a is designed to connect seamlessly with other devices, whether it's for sharing files, connecting to smart home systems, or using it as a personal hotspot. This chapter covers the various ways you can connect and integrate your Pixel 9a with other devices.

## Connecting Pixel 9a to a TV or Projector Using Chromecast

Chromecast lets you cast content from your Pixel 9a to a compatible TV or projector. This is perfect for watching movies, sharing photos, or showing presentations.

### Steps to Use Chromecast:

1. Connect your TV or projector to the **Chromecast** device and make sure it's set up properly.

2. On your Pixel 9a, swipe down the **Quick Settings** menu and tap **Cast**.

3. Select your Chromecast-enabled device from the list of available options.

4. Once connected, you can start casting content from compatible apps like YouTube, Netflix, or Google Photos.

**Tip**: Ensure both your Pixel 9a and Chromecast are connected to the same Wi-Fi network.

## Using the Google Pixel 9a as a Hotspot

You can use your Pixel 9a as a **mobile hotspot** to share your phone's internet connection with other devices, such as a laptop or tablet.

## Steps to Set Up a Mobile Hotspot:

1. Go to **Settings** > **Network & internet** > **Hotspot & tethering**.

2. Tap on **Wi-Fi hotspot** and toggle it on.

3. Customize your hotspot settings, such as the network name and password, by tapping **Hotspot settings**.

4. Once set up, other devices can connect to the hotspot using the Wi-Fi network name and password.

**Tip**: Be mindful of your data usage if you're using mobile data, as this can quickly add up when multiple devices are connected.

## Setting Up USB OTG to Connect External Devices

USB OTG (On-The-Go) allows you to connect external devices like a keyboard, mouse, USB drive, or game controller to your Pixel 9a using a USB cable and an OTG adapter.

## Steps to Use USB OTG:

1. Plug the OTG adapter into the USB-C port of your Pixel 9a.

2. Connect the external device (e.g., a USB drive or keyboard) to the other end of the OTG adapter.

3. Your Pixel 9a should automatically recognize the device and allow you to use it or transfer data.

**Tip**: Some external devices may require additional apps or software to work with your Pixel 9a.

## Pairing Pixel 9a with Wearables (Google Fit, Wear OS Devices)

Your Pixel 9a can sync with various wearable devices, such as smartwatches and fitness trackers, to help you stay connected and track your health.

## Steps to Pair with Wear OS Devices:

1. Open the **Wear OS by Google** app on your Pixel 9a.

2. Follow the on-screen prompts to pair your Pixel 9a with your Wear OS device (such as a Google Pixel Watch or other Wear OS smartwatches).

3. During the pairing process, make sure Bluetooth is turned on, and follow the instructions to complete the connection.

Tip: Make sure your wearable device is charged and within Bluetooth range of your Pixel 9a during the pairing process.

## Sharing Files Using Nearby Share

Nearby Share is a fast, easy way to send files, links, and photos between Android devices that are nearby, without needing an internet connection.

### Steps to Share Files with Nearby Share:

1. Open the file you want to share (such as a photo or document).

2. Tap the **Share** icon and select **Nearby Share** from the list of sharing options.

3. Your Pixel 9a will scan for nearby devices. Select the device you want to share with.

4. The other device will receive a prompt to accept the file transfer. Once accepted, the file will be sent.

**Tip**: Ensure that both devices have **Nearby Share** enabled and that they are within Bluetooth range of each other.

## Using Android Auto in Your Car

Android Auto allows you to connect your Pixel 9a to your car's infotainment system to access apps, navigation, and communication features while driving.

## Steps to Set Up Android Auto:

1. Make sure your car's system supports Android Auto and that it's connected via USB or Bluetooth.

2. Download and install the **Android Auto** app from the Google Play Store (if not already installed).

3. Connect your Pixel 9a to your car using a USB cable (or wirelessly, if supported).

4. Follow the prompts to give Android Auto access to the necessary permissions, such as location and contacts.

5. Once connected, you can access Google Maps, play music, make calls, and more directly from your car's infotainment screen.

**Tip**: Android Auto is designed for safer use while driving. Use voice commands to control features and minimize distractions.

# Chapter 15: Troubleshooting and FAQs

This chapter provides solutions to common issues you may encounter with your Google Pixel 9a. If you're facing any problems, try the following troubleshooting steps before seeking further help.

## Common Issues and Fixes (Wi-Fi Problems, App Crashes, etc.)

### Wi-Fi Problems:

- **Problem**: Wi-Fi is not connecting or keeps disconnecting.

    - **Solution**: Restart your router and your Pixel 9a. If the issue persists, forget the Wi-Fi network in **Settings** > **Network & internet** > **Wi-Fi**, and then reconnect.

## App Crashes:

- **Problem**: Apps keep crashing or freezing.

  - **Solution**: Try force-stopping the app from **Settings** > **Apps**. If the issue continues, uninstall and reinstall the app.

## What to Do if Your Pixel 9a Freezes or is Unresponsive

If your Pixel 9a becomes unresponsive or freezes, try the following:

## Steps to Force Restart:

1. Press and hold the **Power button** and **Volume Down** button simultaneously for about 10 seconds.

2. Your phone will restart, and any minor issues causing the freeze should be resolved.

**Tip**: If this doesn't work, consider performing a factory reset as a last resort (covered in the next section).

## Restoring Your Google Pixel 9a to Factory Settings

If you're experiencing persistent issues or planning to sell or give away your phone, performing a factory reset can restore your phone to its original state.

### Steps to Perform a Factory Reset:

1. Go to **Settings** > **System** > **Reset options**.

2. Tap on **Erase all data (factory reset)**.

3. Confirm the action and follow the prompts to erase all data on your device.

**Warning**: A factory reset will delete all your personal data from the phone, so make sure to back up your data before proceeding.

- Delete unnecessary files or apps.

- Move files to **Google Drive** or an SD card (if supported).

- Use the **Files app** to manage and clear cache data.

## What to Do if Your Phone is Not Charging
**Solution:**

- Check if the charging cable and adapter are working properly. Try using a different cable or charger.

- Inspect the charging port for debris or dust. Clean it gently if needed.

- If charging still doesn't work, perform a **soft reset** (hold the power button for 10 seconds) and try charging again.

## Contacting Google Support
If the issues persist or you need assistance with advanced troubleshooting, you can contact Google Support.

**How to Contact Google Support:**

1. Go to **Settings** > **Help & feedback**.

2. Tap **Contact us** to access the support page and connect with a Google representative.

# Chapter 16: Software Updates and Maintenance

Keeping your Pixel 9a updated with the latest software ensures that your device is secure and running efficiently. In this chapter, we will guide you through the update process and general maintenance tips.

## How to Check for Software Updates

To ensure your phone is running the latest version of Android and security patches, check for software updates regularly.

## Steps to Check for Updates:

1. Go to **Settings** > **System** > **Software update**.

2. Your phone will check for updates. If an update is available, tap **Download and install**.

**Tip**: Keep your Pixel 9a connected to Wi-Fi and charge it while downloading updates.

## Installing System Updates and Security Patches

System updates not only improve performance but also include critical security patches that protect your device from vulnerabilities.

### Steps to Install Updates:

1. When an update is available, tap on **Download and install**.

2. Follow the prompts to install the update. Your phone may restart during the process.

## Understanding Pixel 9a's Update Schedule

Google provides regular software updates for the Pixel 9a, typically every month for security patches and at least one major Android update per year.

**Tip**: Check Google's official update schedule for more details on when updates are released for your device.

## Clearing Cache and Optimizing System Performance

To maintain smooth performance, periodically clear the system cache and unused apps.

**Steps to Clear Cache:**

1. Go to **Settings** > **Storage**.

2. Tap **Cache data** and select **Clear** to remove temporary files.

**Tip**: Clearing cache won't delete personal data, but it may speed up certain apps.

## Factory Reset Instructions and When to Do It

A factory reset can be performed if you're experiencing issues that can't be fixed by regular troubleshooting, or when you're preparing to sell your device.

## Keeping Apps Up to Date

Ensure your apps are up to date to benefit from new features and bug fixes.

## Steps to Update Apps:

1. Open the **Google Play Store**.

2. Tap the **Menu** icon (three lines) > **My apps & games**.

3. Tap **Update all** to update your installed apps.

# Chapter 17: Using Google Services

Google provides a range of services designed to enhance your Pixel 9a experience. This chapter will cover how to sync your accounts, use Google Maps, and access other services like Google Pay.

## Syncing Google Contacts, Calendar, and Gmail

Your Pixel 9a automatically syncs Google Contacts, Calendar, and Gmail for seamless integration across devices.

## Steps to Sync:

1. Go to **Settings** > **Google** > **Sync**.

2. Toggle on **Contacts**, **Calendar**, and **Gmail** to sync your data across devices.

## Using Google Maps for Navigation and Location Sharing

Google Maps is your go-to app for navigation and sharing your location with friends and family.

### Steps to Use Google Maps:

1. Open the **Google Maps** app.

2. Enter your destination and tap **Directions** to start navigation.

3. You can also share your real-time location with others via the app.

## Accessing Google Drive and Google Docs

Google Drive is your cloud storage for documents, photos, and files. Google Docs lets you create, edit, and share documents online.

### Steps to Use Google Drive:

1. Open the **Google Drive** app to access your files.

2. Tap + to upload files or create new documents using **Google Docs**.

## Setting Up Google Pay and Managing Payment Methods

Google Pay lets you make secure payments with your phone. You can also store loyalty cards and tickets.

### Steps to Set Up Google Pay:

1. Download and open the **Google Pay** app.

2. Add a payment method by following the on-screen instructions.

## Using Google Home App for Smart Home Control

With the Google Home app, you can manage and control all your smart home devices from one place.

### Steps to Use Google Home:

1. Open the **Google Home** app.

2. Follow the prompts to set up and control your smart devices.

## Exploring Google Stadia for Gaming

Google Stadia is a cloud gaming service that allows you to play games directly from your Pixel 9a without downloading.

## Steps to Use Google Stadia:

1. Download the **Stadia** app from the Google Play Store.

2. Browse through available games, select one, and start playing directly from the cloud.

That's the end of this comprehensive guide. You're now equipped to get the most out of your Pixel 9a!

www.ingramcontent.com/pod-product-compliance
Lightning Source LLC
LaVergne TN
LVHW052301060326
832902LV00021B/3650